# Glacier
# National Park

*John Hamilton*

National Parks

VISIT US AT

WWW.ABDOPUB.COM

Published by ABDO Publishing Company, 4940 Viking Drive, Suite 622, Edina, Minnesota 55435.

Copyright ©2005 by Abdo Consulting Group, Inc. International copyrights reserved in all countries.

No part of this book may be reproduced in any form without written permission from the publisher.

ABDO & Daughters™ is a trademark and logo of ABDO Publishing Company.

Printed in the United States.

Editor: Paul Joseph

Graphic Design: John Hamilton

All photos and illustrations by John Hamilton, except Great Northern Railway, p. 10 (painting by

Winold Reiss) and National Park Service, p. 7 (map of Glacier National Park), p. 10 (portrait of

George Bird Grinnell), p. 24 (Robert Fire), p. 25 (forest fire), p. 26 (fire at side of road).

**Library of Congress Cataloging-in-Publication Data**

Hamilton, John, 1959–
    Glacier National Park / John Hamilton.
       p. cm. — (National parks)
       Includes index.
      Summary: Discusses the history of this national park, its geological features, plant and animal life,
visiting the park, and efforts to preserve it.
     ISBN 1-59197-425-9
     1. Glacier National Park (Mont.)—Juvenile literature. [1. Glacier National Park (Mont.)
2. National parks and reserves.] I. Title. II. National parks (ABDO Publishing Company)

    F737.G5H35 2005
    917.86'52—dc21

                                 2003044375

# Contents

*Mountain goats and hikers share a path near Logan Pass, along the Continental Divide.*

**Mountain Wildflowers** bloom in Glacier National Park.

# The Glacier Experience

The vastness of Glacier National Park can be an overwhelming experience. As you approach by car from the east, after crossing hundreds of miles of eastern Montana's rolling plains, craggy mountains suddenly rise up and kiss the sky. Dense forests crowd the shoulders of these seemingly limitless peaks, eventually giving way to alpine meadows, tundra, then sheer rock as the mountains rise higher and higher.

Even the weather pauses before crossing over Glacier. The Continental Divide, which traverses the park, rises so high that clouds are sometimes held back, as if a giant stone hand is blocking the way. One side of the park might be bright and sunny, while the other is cloaked in dense fog, or even thunderstorms. It certainly makes for dramatic, often breathtaking, scenery.

In Glacier, there are no iconic, one-of-a-kind views associated with many other national parks. There is no Old Faithful geyser, no stunning Yosemite valley, no majestic Grand Canyon rim overlook. Instead, Glacier embraces an entire ecosystem, over one million acres (404,686 hectares) of forests, 650 lakes, glaciers, and alpine meadows preserved for the enjoyment of future generations. So much is here to be discovered: Taken as a whole, Glacier is every bit as awe-inspiring as those other national parks. Once visited, it cannot be forgotten.

*Mountain goats are often seen along the Highline Trail, a high-altitude route that runs parallel to the Continental Divide.*

Glacier National Park was established in 1910. It preserves an intact ecosystem, the largest in the lower 48 states. It can easily be visited by car, but it is a paradise for hikers. Over 700 miles (1,127 km) of maintained trails crisscross Glacier, taking visitors to hidden valleys and jewel-like lakes among the 175 mountains in the park, the tallest of which, Mt. Cleveland, stands at 10,448 feet (3,185 m). Animal lovers are rewarded as well: Over 70 species of mammals are found in the park, including endangered wolves and grizzly bears. There are more than 260 species of birds. More than 1,200 kinds of plants grow in the mountain landscape.

More than 350 man-made structures in the park are listed on the National Register of Historic Sites. The Great Northern Railway built backcountry chalets in the early 1900's. Two of them, Granite Park and Sperry, have been designated National Historic Landmarks. Still in use today, they can only be reached by hiking or by horseback, making for a memorable adventure.

For people who prefer sightseeing by car instead of hiking, the park does not disappoint. The magnificent Going-to-the-Sun Road winds its way through the middle of Glacier. The road is a highlight for most park visitors. It is a steep and narrow 50-mile (80-km) east-west route, but there are many places to get out and enjoy jaw-dropping vistas. At Logan Pass the road crosses the Continental Divide, 6,646 feet (2,026 m) above sea level. A visitor center at the top makes a good base for high-altitude hikes, including a trek to nearby Hidden Lake, which contains glimmering azure water surrounded by soaring mountain peaks.

The Glacier area contains an ecosystem unrestricted by the boundaries formed by people. Glacier National Park sits in the northwest part of Montana, its northern boundary forming the international border with Alberta, Canada. On the other side of the border sits Waterton Lakes National Park, Canada's share of this incredible natural habitat.

**Hidden Lake** is a short walk from Logan Pass Visitor Center.

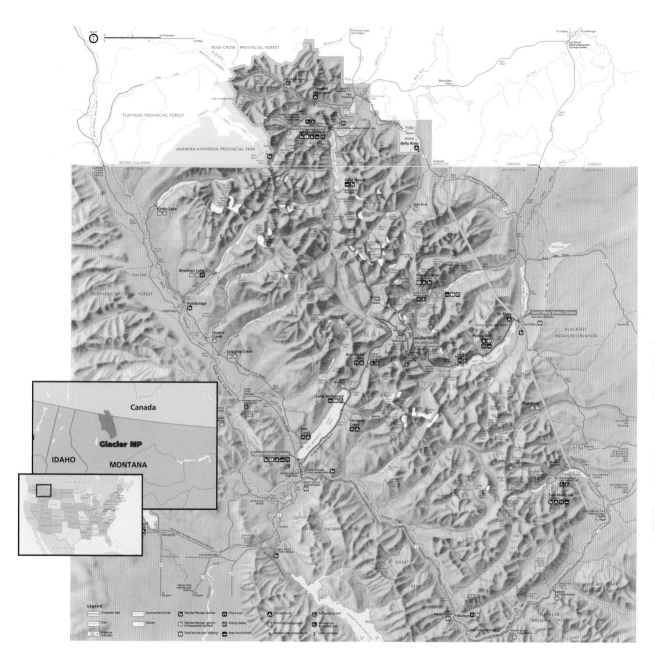

In 1932, the two neighboring parks were combined to form Waterton-Glacier International Peace Park. The two parks are administered separately, but they cooperate in managing wildlife and scientific research. The U.S. and Canadian governments want to make the park "a symbol of permanent peace and friendship."

Despite industrial development in neighboring areas that threatens Glacier's habitats, the world's first International Peace Park is working hard to preserve a unique mountain wilderness for generations to come.

*"... the best care-killing scenery on the continent."* Naturalist John Muir

# Glacier's History

*George Bird Grinnell played a major part in establishing Glacier as a national park.*

Native people have lived in the Glacier National Park area for thousands of years. Archaeological discoveries point to a human presence dating as far back as 10,000 years ago.

In the early 1800s, French, English, and Spanish trappers came to find beaver pelts. By this time, Blackfeet Indians lived on the plains east of the Rockies. Salish and Kootenai Indians lived in valleys to the west, sometimes crossing over the mountains to the eastern plains to hunt buffalo. Roads and hiking trails now trace the paths these peoples used to travel through the area.

The intrusion of Europeans forced the native peoples onto reservations. Trappers and miners exploited the natural resources of the area throughout the late 1800s. Miners were especially eager to find copper and gold. The Great Northern Railway completed a crossing over Marias Pass in 1892, further opening up the area for development.

Early explorers and sightseers, including rancher Fredrick Godsal and conservationist George Bird Grinnell, urged the government to preserve the spectacular scenery and animals found in the area.

In 1910, President William Howard Taft signed a law creating Glacier National Park, the country's 10th national park.

*In the late 1920s, artist Winold Reiss painted a series of Blackfeet Indian portraits for the Great Northern Railway, which the company used in calendars and postcards to attract tourists to the Glacier area.*

Like steam pouring over the lip of a cup of hot tea, a cloud bank (above) streams over the Highline Trail near Logan Pass. The trail leads to one of two remaining chalets built by the Great Northern Railway in the early 1920s. The Swiss-style Many Glacier Hotel (below) was built by the railroad in 1915 to promote tourism, and is still in use today.

# Geology

The landscape of Glacier National Park didn't always contain soaring mountains. Shallow seas once covered the flat countryside. Starting about 1.6 billion years ago, during the Proterozoic age, tiny pieces of eroded earth called sediments were washed to the bottom of the sea. Layers and layers of this sediment material—sand, clay, calcite—were deposited and compressed for millions of years. The resulting rock is what we see exposed in the park today. But how were the mountains created? The mountains in Glacier National Park are the result of what geologists call the Lewis Overthrust Fault. It is the reason why Glacier's mountains appear to rise up so abruptly from Montana's eastern plains.

The surface of our planet is always moving and shifting. The Earth's crust is divided into several massive sections called tectonic plates. These solid plates float around on layers of hotter, more fluid material, changing position over millions of years. Two of these tectonic plates began colliding 170 million years ago, during the second half of the Mesozoic Era, the age of the dinosaurs. Millions of years of geologic uplifting eventually formed the Rocky Mountains.

In the Glacier area, a huge section of earth cracked about 75 million years ago. A giant rock wedge many miles thick and several hundred miles long lifted and

slid eastward about 50 miles (80 km). This overthrusting wedge became the mountains that exist today in Glacier National Park.

*Mount Oberlin as seen from Going-to-the-Sun Road, approaching Logan Pass and the Continental Divide.*

"**Old Man (Napi)** *came from the south, making the mountains, the prairies, and the forests as he passed along, making the birds and animals also. He traveled northward making things as he went, putting red paint in the ground here and there—arranging the world as we see it today.*" Blackfeet Creation Legend

# Glaciers

Glacier National Park is named for the massive ice formations that helped shape the park's landscape. Glaciers lie up against the sides of mountains. They are formed when more snow accumulates in winter than melts in summer. The snow builds up into thick layers that are compacted into ice. Ice near the top of the glacier is hard, but pressure from above keeps ice at the bottom flexible. This allows gravity to slowly pull the entire sheet of ice downhill.

There are 37 glaciers in the park today. About 20,000 years ago, the climate was much cooler and wetter. Huge glaciers formed in the park. Valleys were filled with ice thousands of feet thick, so that only the very tops of the tallest mountains stuck out. These giant rivers of ice ground across the landscape, sculpting the steep mountains and deep U-shaped valleys that we see today. As the Earth's climate warmed and the ancient ice melted, many deep lakes were left behind.

Glaciers carve several unique features that can be seen today in the park. When glaciers surround a mountain, they can erode it so that all that is left is a tooth-like horn. Mt. Reynolds, which can be seen from Logan Pass, on Going-to-the-Sun Road, is an example of a horn.

*Mt. Reynolds, which towers over the Logan Pass visitor center, is a good example of a glacial horn.*

**Jackson Glacier** can be seen from Going-to-the-Sun Road.

**Lake McDonald** is the result of a glacial moraine.

*Garden Wall is an example of an arête, a long, narrow ridge left behind when two glaciers grind away at opposite sides of a mountain.*

When two glaciers work on opposite sides of a mountain, they may leave behind a long, narrow ridge. This is called an arête, which is French for fish-bone. From Logan Pass, you can see a good example of an arête at Garden Wall, which looms over visitors to the north. Like an impenetrable fortress, Garden Wall separates two major valleys in the park, Lake McDonald Valley and Many Glacier Valley.

Cirques are steep-sided valleys that once contained glaciers. Very often sub-alpine lakes are contained in cirques when the glaciers eventually melt away. These areas look like a giant has used an enormous ice cream scoop upon the landscape.

A moraine is a collection of rock and debris that forms at the head and sides of a glacier as it makes its slow, grinding descent. The debris wall at the front of a glacier is called a terminal moraine. Sometimes when the glacier melts, the moraines at the head and sides act like a dam, creating a narrow lake. Lake McDonald was created by a terminal moraine and is the largest lake in the park.  It measures 10 miles (16 km) long and is over 400 feet (122 m) deep.

A hanging valley occurs when a small glacier comes down a side valley, like a river's tributary, and joins with a larger glacier. The small glacier cannot cut as deep a valley as the main glacier. When the glaciers melt and recede, a small valley is left high up on the mountainside. These hanging valleys are very common in the park.

The glaciers left today in the park work the same way as the glaciers of the past. They are continually reshaping the landscape. However, changes in the Earth's climate have caused glaciers all over the world to shrink at an alarming rate. Scientists blame global warming for the park not getting enough snow during winter to replenish the ice that melts in summer. According to the United States Geological Survey, at the current rate of rapid melting, all of the park's glaciers could disappear by the year 2030.

# Going-to-the-Sun Road

In the early days of Glacier National Park, visitors usually arrived by train, then stayed at hotels or small backcountry lodges, called chalets. These were built by the Great Northern Railway to boost tourism in the area. Seeing the interior of the park, however, meant several days of hiking or horseback riding. Demand for a road that led through the mountains increased as tourism grew.

Going-to-the-Sun Road was completed in 1932, after 11 years of hard work. The road's construction is a marvel of engineering. For 12 miles (19 km) of the road's 50-mile (80-km) length, workers carved a pathway right out of a mountainside, the Garden Wall, which was an extremely dangerous task. A few workers died in falls or were struck by falling rocks.

Today the road is a National Historic Landmark, one of the most scenic routes in America. The paved, two-lane east-west road opens Glacier's spectacular scenery to hundreds of thousands of tourists who visit the park each year.

*"There is no highway which will give the seer, the lover of grandeur of the Creator's handiwork, more thrills, more genuine satisfaction deep in his being, than will a trip over this road."* Montana Governor Frank H. Cooney, Dedication of Going-to-the-Sun Road, July 15, 1933

**Haystack Falls** is one of many sights along Going-to-the-Sun Road.

# Wildlife in Glacier

Glacier National Park is a great place to watch animals in their natural setting. It is one of the largest intact ecosystems in the country. Because of the variety of terrain, it's common to spot moose, elk, deer, beaver, mountain goats, golden eagles, and bighorn sheep in a single visit to the park. But it's the big carnivores that people are most interested in.

During the late 1980's, wolves returned to Glacier after a 50-year absence. Black bears inhabit the woods, but the park is more famous for its population of threatened grizzly bears. Grizzlies can be huge, weighing up to 600 pounds (272 kg).

For most park visitors, it's a rare treat to spot a grizzly roaming the high country, or foraging for huckleberries along streams or hillsides. For hikers, however, coming face to face with a grizzly bear can be unnerving. People have been killed by bears in the past, but it's usually not the bears' fault.

Jennifer Lay, a National Park Service interpreter from Austin, Texas, says that most bear trouble is caused by humans. "You don't want to surprise a bear," she says, "especially not a mamma with cubs." She advises hikers to talk loudly, or wear special bells around their ankles, to avoid surprising bears and causing confrontations. "Usually if they hear you coming, bears will just get out of the way."

During the summer of 2004, a man was attacked by a bear just outside the park. He was in his tent sleeping when the bear swiped at him, slashing through the tent fabric and cutting his face and neck. It turned out that the man had stored food in his tent, never a good idea in bear country.

Mountain goats (above) are often found in the higher elevations in the park. This one was spotted on a narrow mountain path called the Highline Trail, which runs parallel to the Continental Divide in the central part of Glacier. Hoary marmots (below left) and ptarmigan (below right) have excellent camouflage for blending in with the area's rocks.

Garden Wall (above) looms over a stand of trees near the Continental Divide. The Logan Pass Visitor Center is a good place to view Garden Wall. The small island on Upper Saint Mary Lake (below) is one of the most photographed spots in the park.

*A horse wrangler brings in a herd near the shores of Swiftcurrent Lake. A 2.6-mile (4.2-km) loop trail around the lake takes visitors through spruce-fir and lodgepole pine forests. Frigid mountain water cascades through McDonald Falls (below).*

# Fire!

Forest fires are a natural part of the environment. Even though it seems fires scorch everything to cinders, this is not true. Fires are crucial to a forest staying healthy. By clearing out deadwood and other organic material, fire gives other plants room to grow. Forests that experience regular periods of fire tend to be more resistant to drought and insect invasions. Also, the intensity of future fires is reduced. In forests where well-meaning humans continually suppress fires, dead matter collects on the forest floor until it becomes a giant tinderbox. The resulting fire is much more severe, damaging trees that otherwise would have survived a smaller forest fire.

Glacier National Park averages 14 fires each summer. Most are caused by lightning strikes. Since 1988, about 5,000 acres (2,023 hectares) have been burned each year. Some of these fires are very small, and most park visitors are never even aware of them. Unless the fires threaten to burn out of control, or threaten lives or important park structures, they are allowed to burn themselves out. This shapes the landscape of the park the way nature intended.

*The Robert Fire started in late July, 2003, and burned much of Apgar Mountain.*

**Forest fires** help ecosystems stay healthy and diverse.

In the summer of 2003, several fires swept through Glacier. These were major fires that forced the evacuation of parts of the park and nearby communities.

The Smith family, from Idaho, visit the park each summer. They witnessed one of 2003's major blazes, the Robert Fire, while picnicking on the south shore of Lake McDonald. Across the lake, they watched as the fire line advanced over Howe Ridge. "You could see the wall of flame hundreds of feet high come over the ridge," said Ted Smith. "Smoke covered the sky. It was like nighttime in the middle of the day. We could see hot embers falling on the lake. Ahead of the fire, you could see individual trees light up like matches, and then join the main fire. It took only about an hour for the whole side of the mountain to go up in flames." The Smiths were soon escorted to safety by park rangers.

The fires of 2003 burned over 135,000 acres (54,633 hectares) of forest. It was the most significant fire season in the history of the park. Some people feared Glacier would be a ruined cinder, but most of the park remained untouched, and the parts that did burn are already starting to regenerate in the ecosystem's continuing cycle of growth, death, and rebirth.

In August 2003, Montana's U.S. Senator Conrad Burns toured the aftermath of the fires. "One never forgets the sights or the smell" of the devastation of a forest fire, said Burns, who once was a firefighter for the United States Forest Service. "I want people to know Glacier is open for business, and while they have seen the damage of fire, there is much natural beauty and splendor for all to enjoy.

*The summer of 2003 was the most significant fire season in the history of Glacier National Park.*

The fire-damaged McDonald Creek area (above), as seen from the Loop section of Going-to-the-Sun Road. After only one year, the forest floor of even the most badly burned areas is beginning to generate new growth (below).

# Future Challenges

Glacier National Park is only part of a larger ecosystem that occupies millions of acres of surrounding countryside. Wild animals, especially the larger carnivores, wander in and out of the park unaware of the artificial boundaries created by humans. When surrounding lands are altered or developed, the entire ecosystem is stressed, endangering many species of plants and animals.

Today, in the land surrounding Glacier, strip-mining and oil, gas, housing, and logging projects threaten to disrupt this fragile balance. The National Park Service has partnered with conservation groups, as well as the Blackfeet Indian Reservation, to work with private companies in order to protect the Glacier ecosystem.

Glacier National Park has changed often in the past. During the last 100 years we've recognized a great need to preserve our ever-shrinking wilderness lands. But we also now recognize the importance of fire and other natural processes that alter the landscape. As the National Park Service says, "Through all the many changes in how people have used the land, one thing has not changed: this remains one of the world's great places, worthy of special care and lasting respect."

*Overcrowding is a growing problem in Glacier National Park, as well as many other national parks.*

**Wildflowers** growing near Logan Pass.

# Glossary

### Continental Divide

A ridge of the Rocky Mountains in North America. Water flowing east of the divide eventually goes to the Atlantic Ocean. Water flowing west goes to the Pacific Ocean.

### Ecosystem

A biological community of animals, plants, and bacteria, all of whom live together in the same physical or chemical environment.

### Forest Service

The United States Department of Agriculture (USDA) Forest Service was started in 1905 to manage public lands in national forests and grasslands. The Forest Service today oversees an area of 191 million acres (77.3 million hectares), which is an amount of land about the same size as Texas. In addition to protecting and managing America's public lands, the Forest Service also conducts forestry research and helps many state government and private forestry programs.

### Geological Survey

The United States Geological Survey was created in 1879. It is an independent science agency that is part of the Department of the Interior. It researches and collects facts about the land of the United States, giving us a better understanding of our natural resources.

### Glacier

A glacier is often called a river of ice. It is made of thick sheets of ice and snow. Glaciers slowly move downhill, scouring and smoothing the landscape.

### Great Northern Railway

The Great Northern Railway began in 1889 with the merger of several existing railroad companies. Great Northern was the dream of James J. Hill, who was called the "Empire Builder" for his ability to create successful businesses. His railway line eventually stretched across the northern U.S., from St. Paul, Minnesota to Seattle, Washington, skirting Glacier National Park along the way. To attract tourists to the Glacier area (most of whom, of course, would ride the Great Northern Railway to get there), Hill constructed a number of hotels and chalets in the park. Several are still in use today.

### TEMPERATE ZONE
A moderate climate zone that is found between the tropics and the polar circles.

### TUNDRA
Tundra is normally thought of as the vast, almost treeless plains of the Arctic regions. Some mountains are so high and cold that tundra conditions exist on their upper elevations.

*A Colombian ground squirrel watches from his burrow as hikers pass by along a fog-shrouded Highline Trail.*

# Index